Confessions
of an
INTERNET MODEL

How I Succeeded on the WORLD WIDE WEB

SHANTELLE!

Printcess Publishing
PO Box 50
Venice, CA 90294
www.printcesspublishing.com

Second Edition

ISBN-13:
978-0997798395

ISBN-10:
0997798394

Hello, I am Shantelle of Shantelle.net! Enjoy my Book!

TO MY MOM:

I'm dedicating this book to my wonderful Mother, Diana! My MOM is a Breast Cancer SURVIVOR and the strongest woman I know! I LOVE YOU,Mom! Thanks for always being there for me!

.

Printcess
publishing

FABULOUS TABLE OF CONTENTS

1	Less is More	1
2	Put Your Best Face Forward	6
3	Ask & Answer	10
4	Be Aware	24
5	Picture Perfect	32
6	Follow the Leader	40
7	Have Fun	44
8	Positivity	50
9	My Best Accessories	67
10	Coast 2 Coast	70
11	Make Progress Everyday	74

AWARD WINNING CAST

Thanks to my family for always being there for me!
I LOVE YOU VERY MUCH!

Oly: There isn't enough space in this book to thank "YOU!" Oly, you're an angel! THANK YOU for introducing me to the Internet & most of all, being the best friend ever! Teamwork makes the dream work! ☺

Jimmy: My Mentor! You motivate, inspire, and guide me! You really are Mr. Wonderful! Your students are so lucky!

Bookman: The books you send me helped me realize my dream of becoming a writer, THANK YOU!

John B. : Your postcards allowed me to travel the world! Your photos made me laugh out loud & become a traveler myself!

Farouk: Thanks for making sure I got out to celebrate and have fun at the hottest reggae spots and events in town, always VIP style!

Fulvia: Thanks for guiding me through my first time in New York and being a perfect example of how to live life to the fullest!

Jake: Thanks for introducing me to online publishing sites & copyright info!

Leslie: Thanks for being such a wonderful and genuine friend & shopping buddy! Cheers to many more Girl's Nights Out & In!

FANS All over the World: YOU ROCK! Thanks for keeping me going each day! Your support and loyalty are greatly appreciated!

Rick Segal: Thanks for emailing me back and teach me how to Laugh & Get Rich! YOUR ROCK! I loved your book

Mary Foley: Thanks for showing me the ropes of becoming a Bodacious Woman, outrageously in charge of My Life & Lovin' it!"
Your book was so much fun to read!

Tori Hartman: Thanks for teaching me to be "Fabulous.. Unlocking my perfect personal style!" Your book was a blast to read!

Photographer Steve Diet Goedde: Thanks for making my dream come true and publishing me as a model in your fabulous book!

Bench Warmer: Thanks for promoting me on your beautiful trading cards and capturing me on the red carpet for my first time, all by myself!

INTRODUCTION

*"Imagining what you want as if it
already exists opens the door to letting it happen."*
Shakti Gawan Author of Creative Visualization

Hello Everyone, I'm Shantelle of www.Shantelle.net!

I'm a Model in sunny southern California. I decided to write Confessions of an Internet Model, because I get so many emails each day from aspiring models wanting advice and wondering how I got my start with modeling. So I'm here today to tell you my personal story. I wanted to put together a book on how I became successful and fulfilled several of my dreams of being a model by promoting myself on the World Wide Web. I'm telling my story to inspire others to get out there and make their dreams come to life. Trust me, DREAMS do come true & it's up to you to MAKE IT HAPPEN!!

Barbie Doll Central

Okay, so it starts here! Growing up, I've always had a fascination for Barbie Dolls, fashion, magazines, models, & clothes, clothes, clothes! When I was a little girl, my mom used to always buy me so many clothes & make me so many outfits. I was always in style. I even had several of the same outfits in numerous colors. I always had my own style, not really like anyone else. In fact, when I look back at old photos, I definitely had a style of my own, out of this world that is.

I remember when I was a little girl, I used to absolutely LOVE McDonald's; for my birthday my Mom made me a cute little yellow and red dress, colors that Ronald McDonald wore, for my birthday at McDonald's. I was so happy! When I look back at that dress, it brings back memories of how much I loved that outfit. ☺

Growing up in a creative family must have definitely sparked my interest in the entertainment world. So naturally, one day, I decided that I wanted to become a Model. So, somehow I got my mom to send me to a very well-known Modeling School. After my personal experience, I would not recommend modeling school to anyone. I learned absolutely nothing. I mean, I grew up knowing how to walk. Did I really need to pay someone $2,500 to learn? I remember in one class session, we learned how to put on makeup. Oh NO! The instructors did not even have makeup for my skin tone. Huh? I was in shock and they completely used the wrong colors on my face. It was a nightmare. In fact, I looked like a clown. Til this day, I'm just learning how to do my own makeup, go figure.

In another modeling class, we had our first photo shoot and these were the worst photos of my career. Okay, so maybe I did not know how to pose, didn't know my best camera angles, etc. - but looking back, oh my goodness! Why did they give me prints of those horrible photos and make me pay for them? The lighting was completely wrong and the wardrobe was hideous, ick! Couldn't somebody have helped me for $2,500? I know the slogan says "Be a model or just look like one!" Couldn't someone have at least just made me look like a Model for one day? What a wild experience!

Hollywood Dreaming

After graduating from modeling school, I was on my way to Supermodel Stardom. Okay, so at least I thought. First off, I was definitely in the wrong place to start my modeling career. There were hardly any modeling agencies in my hometown of Washington. Okay, so maybe I made my modeling debut in a local fashion newspaper from doing a fashion show and once again appearing in my college brochure as a Cheerleader. Go Team Go! After graduating college, I decided to move to L.A.. Being the dreamer that I've always been, L.A. was definitely the place I wanted to live. I remember sitting in my room in Washington, just dreaming about being able to hang out with the girls on 90210 or Sweet Valley High. I would get to shop on Melrose or maybe even live on Melrose like the TV show & I would get to go to the beach every single day. Woo-Hoo! I couldn't wait to go shopping on Rodeo Drive and see all the cool celebrities. I had a dream that my career would take off right away, because I was in a town where you could get discovered. Also, I wanted to move to L.A., because I wanted to get away from the Rainy Seattle weather, become independent, and live in constant sunshine 24/7. Score!

Since I didn't know anyone in L.A., I decided to apply to Fashion School. After all, I did love fashion. Maybe modeling and fashion would tie in together to creating my successful career. It does make sense, a Model who is also a Fashion Designer, right? How cool would that be? I could model for my own clothing line. PERFECT! I had never been great in sketching; in fact, I knew nothing at all about how to draw. However, I put my pencil to paper right away, let my imagination run wild & sent my application off to fashion school. Which I might add, I did get accepted to. I was so happy!

Driven

Off to L.A. I went. The fashion school had found roommates in L.A. for me to stay with. I was so excited. I remember arriving at LAX and being in complete awe of the palm trees & the promise of constant sunshine. I had finally taken the steps to making my dreams come true. Sunshine and Modeling. I had arrived. Fashion school did not work out and I found that out after a year & $5,000 later. Fashion school was definitely NOT for me. I didn't like to sew, didn't really want to learn to sew and I could not draw for the life of me. I was so shocked when I received such a low grade for a sketch I had done for a class. How did this happen? I did fantastic in college & had already earned my degree in Political Science. How was it possible that I was not succeeding in fashion school? After deciding to leave fashion school, I was off to open calls at a number of modeling agencies.

After all, everyone had always told me I looked like a model and now I was in the right place, L.A. I received rejection after rejection when I attended agency open calls at Elite, Ford, Wilhelmina, Next, Click, CED & more. In fact, I even kept a journal of my experience. Hmm...maybe I should publish this journal one day. I might have to make that happen. Okay, back to the story. The agencies said that I wasn't tall enough, my photos were not good enough, I should work with their photographers (Yeah right for a totally ridiculous price), or they already represented someone who had my look. I was exhausted and I just couldn't understand why I wasn't able to find an agency. Unfortunately, I had fallen into the trap of paying one of these totally ridiculous glamour models agencies over $1,500 to shoot with their photographer. I can't even begin to tell you about the end result. My pictures were horrible. In fact, I'm so ashamed of the makeup, wardrobe, and photography that I won't even show you. They made me look like a clown. This had been my last straw of trying to become a model. I was never known to be a quitter, but I was so tired of being rejected and I was getting exhausted from going to so many agencies. What was I to do next?

Discovered

My best friend knew of my dreams to become a model and he suggested that I try the Internet; go online. He mentioned that I should try promoting myself on the Internet to help jumpstart my modeling career. Hmm... I had never even considered the Internet. In fact, I was totally against this from the beginning, because I thought the Internet was a place full of perverts. How could being online possibly help my modeling career? Little did I know, being online would soon change my life! My friend had great technical resources, which supplied me with a computer. He taught me how to build my own website, I learned how to promote online, and now I'm hear to tell you how I succeeded with my modeling career on the world wide web and made my dream come to life! Let me tell you, it feels really good to have accomplished goals that I had set for myself. I have been published as a cover model as well as featured in numerous books, magazines, on trading cards, traveled plenty, won bikini contests, traveled the world as a spokesmodel and worked with several talented photographers & models. I have had the opportunity to meet and work with a lot of amazing and talented people. All of this happened because I did not give up my dream. I found a way to make it happen. With a super crew behind you 100%, anything is possible!

I hope my book inspires everyone to accomplish everything their little hearts desire. YOU have the ability to make your DREAMS COME TO LIFE!

Enjoy my book and be sure to email me and let me know how you liked the book. After all, it's my first and I'm so proud. Now, go out there and make it happen! ☺ NO! Wait, stay and read my book! ☺

"Determination always beats fatigue in the final kick!"
L.A. Marathon Billboard on Wilshire Blvd.

At the Hollywood Book Festival

Photo by Blaze

1

BUILD A SIMPLE WEBSITE
"LESS IS MORE!"

When I began my modeling career, I had been in and out of tons of modeling agencies. Many of them said "NO" because I was not tall enough or I would have to pay them to shoot with their photographers or maybe I looked like someone they currently represented. Whatever the reason of the day was, I would not give up. I was determined to hear a YES from one of the agencies, because I knew my look would fit in somewhere. Then, one day, my friend suggested that I start a website. I said "That's Not Going To Work!" I didn't know anything about the Internet. I thought "A Website?" I don't even know how to use a computer, let alone turn one on at the time. My friend helped me scan a few photos, built me a website, and I was now what they called "ONLINE!! "

"If you build, they will come!"
Field of Dreams Movie

Considering my friend had a busy schedule or what many would call "A LIFE," he was not always able to update my website whenever my heart desired. So being the motivated self-starter that I am, I asked him to show me how to update my own website. I took notes as he taught me step by step. I spent hours and hours at the computer trying to figure out everything, even getting frustrated at times when things didn't work out, because it was a bit overwhelming. I even wanted to throw the computer out of the window a couple of times when I was frustrated. LOL! ☺ Daily practice and several months later, I eventually became great at both using the computer and learning simple design skills. I took his notes and eventually built my own website. Yes, the one and only www.SHANTELLE.net! I was on my way! ☺ Soon after, I started receiving invites to be on other modeling websites, modeling job offers poured in, photographers requesting to work with me, paid photo shoots, and invites to exchange links with other models. Holy cow, it was happening so quickly! Who knew the Internet could help my career take off so fast. I was so happy!

GLAMOUR GIRL TIP

There are several online websites that will host your site for free. Search Google and they will start to appear magically. These sites were very helpful to me, because it gave me step-by-step easy instructions to put my photos online. I was able to choose my website name, color of the site, placement of the photos and everything. I was on a roll!

**Keep in mind that since some of these sites are free, they will promote other banners on your website as well! **

I had now created www.Shantelle.net. Shantelle.com was already taken and the person who owns the name was asking for way too much money for me to purchase it! Besides, .NET was actually really cool, because everybody had .com. Plus, .NET would make me stand out from the bunch, right? Look at me, always seeing the brighter side of things! Growing up, I had never wanted to fit in with a crowd, I was unique, in my own creative way, so this was my way of saying "Hey, this is Me!" I wanted to be different or do things differently, because I knew that it would be what made me unique. I wanted to lead the crowd, not follow, which came natural to me. Maybe I was on to something here.

**There are plenty of websites where you can upload your photos onto an easy to use page and promote yourself for FREE as a Model:

www.onemodelplace.com
www.modelmayhem.com

Rules of Attraction!

After browsing through several online sites, I discovered that the simpler the website, the easier it may be for the client to hire me as a model. A simple website immediately allows the client to see me and make their decision on whether to book me or not. While beautiful websites with flash and music can be amusing, keep in mind that YOU are the main focus here as a Model. I'm not suggesting that you build a "Plain Jane" website, because it's important to also represent your personality and showcase your creativity. Build a website that showcases YOU!

Stay FOCUSED!!

I am saying, however, that sometimes all of the graphics can be distracting and may even take a long time to download, which may cause someone to click off from your website. Not everyone is as patient as you may want them to be and many times, the client is too busy and may not have time to wait for your website to download.

I have also learned valuable advice with photos as well. YOU are the main focus. While a beautiful background and a busy background in photos can be amazing, be careful not to let the background overpower you. Once again, we're not advertising photography, we're advertising our abilities as models and we are the main focus. At this very moment, allow yourself to be the center of attention. Don't let the background get in your way!

Steer clear of the clutter.

Confessions of an Internet Model

Photo by Christine

2

Put Your Best Face Forward.

Only Display Photos Which Represent
The Type of Work You're Looking For!

I've always wondered why so many models always complained of getting so many nasty, inappropriate job inquires or dirty emails and I didn't seem to attract that sort of attention. What made people send inappropriate emails to other models and not me? Aha, the content of their websites or the person sending the email is just a plain old pervert could be the reason.

"Just Do it!"
Nike

It's very important to put photos on your website which REFLECT the sort of modeling work YOU are looking for! If you're getting tons of emails on doing work similar to what is shown on your site, which you're not interested in, then maybe you need to re-evaluate your portfolio and see how you're representing yourself. I always kept my website pretty tame or at least at my own comfort level. It is very important to know what your limits are as far as modeling ahead of time. PLAN ahead! Knowing what you will do and what you won't do needs to be determined before you build your online portfolio and put up your website. YOU always have a choice of doing what feels right for YOU.

Photo by Stars

3

Answer Business Mail Immediately & Ask A Million Questions!!

I used to think that it was good to delay answering my email instead of answering it immediately, because it makes it seem as though I was busy and in demand. WRONG! The only way to stay busy and in demand is to answer your email right away or in a timely manner and discuss the possibilities of booking more work. You live and you learn, right? See, everyone learns from their mistakes, NOBODY is perfect!

I seem to negotiate my bookings very well on my own. I am comfortable making my own deals, rates, & decisions. Sometimes, I find it even better when I handled my bookings instead of letting an agent handle it for me, because that extra 10-20% more that I would make, would be going to an agency instead of me anyway. I get to keep the entire amount. It's also a good idea to note here that although I am great at booking my own modeling work, agencies can often negotiate bookings with bigger clients for more exposure and better pay. You decide what works best for you!

"Sometimes things which seem too good to be true, really can be TRUE!! "

Look at all of the opportunities I could have missed out on if I had waited too long to answer my emails. The following emails were all very time sensitive. I needed to reply right away or I could have missed out and what a shame that would have been.

Be an ANGEL!

GLAMOUR GIRL CASE & POINT #2

Celebrity Golf Tournament : I received an email about a Charity event with all travel expenses paid, room and board to Cabo, Mexico for 4 days for models participating in at least two model activities to raise money for an abused women & children's shelter! I went to the website, everything looked great, celebrities were listed, events were listed, contact info was on the site (Phone Numbers, Location of the Event, Event Coordinator, Emails) and photos of models attending. I was like this is too good to be true! I hesitated for a second, because it seemed almost too good to be true, but sent in my info including a couple of photos. The same day I received an email confirming me for the event along with flight arrangements and all! I was so in shock that I called the event coordinator to make sure it was really true & what do you know, it was totally LEGIT! Imagine that!

When travel arrangements and accommodations are made for me, I always call the hotel, car service and airline to make sure they are in my name and in fact legit. You can never be too sure, you know? I want to make sure things will run smoothly once I arrive and that all of the details are in order.

Just to think, a girlfriend of mine had told me that she heard the event was already to capacity. However, my further inquiry landed me a great trip to Cabo with fellow models and a fantastic time, while raising money for a great cause! This is why I think it's always important to QUESTION Everything! Feel free to ask as many questions as possible. Otherwise, I could have missed out on a fantastic opportunity. Also, if I had waited any longer to reply, the event may have been booked up already.

Here is a photo of me at the Celebrity Golf Tournament charity event at the golf course in Cabo, Mexico! The event raises money for abused women & children's shelters! What a beautiful place & a great cause, right? It's located right next to the beach. See the cute outfit they gave me along with angel wings to wear at the event!

**A completely fun charity event! Models can participate in modeling activities ranging from bikini/lingerie fashion shows, modeling in a swimsuit calendar, auctioning off celebrity items, or assisting at the golf course tournament to raise money and plenty more activities for a great cause all, while having fun in the sun at a resort in Cabo, Mexico. Why not use your popularity for a great cause, right? Haha! I have a blast each year. So far I've been twice and the second time my best girlfriend came along with me. It was also like a little vacation for the both of us, hooray! Also, a way two vacation for FREE each year!

GO for the GOAL!

GLAMOUR GIRL CASE & POINT #3

A Magazine Super Bowl Event in New Orleans, LA: I received an email about an upcoming Super Bowl event taking place in New Orleans, LA. The email was very simple and to the point, but I was happy to see that there was contact info. Maybe a sentence or two and that was the entire email. Although I'm not that crazy about sports, I knew that working at the event and attending the parties with the other models was sure to be a blast & would be a great opportunity for me to network. Once again, I interviewed over the phone with the coordinator in New Jersey, asked a million questions: The location, hotel name, who would be my roommate, other contact/references were supplied (Both Female) and sure enough I received my plane ticket and I was on my way to New Orleans.

GLAMOUR GIRL TIP

I always called my parents to let them know where I was traveling and gave them all of the contact info as well. They always called to check on me whenever I traveled to be sure that everything was okay. Letting at least 1 or 2 people know all of the contact info when you're traveling is very important & a SAFE thing to do in case something happens. I always forwarded my parents the flight info as well! ☺

Knowledge is POWER, SMART GIRLS RULE!

If you're interested in modeling online, I believe it's important to ask all of the necessary questions so that you'll be completely informed about the assignment, like an agent would if you were with an agency. At the start of my modeling career, I have always felt very comfortable booking myself for assignments and I knew the appropriate questions to ask, because I am a very detailed oriented person, plus I've learned from personal experience. It's wise to learn from past experiences, right? I always need to know everything about the modeling job and they have to answer each and every question I ask! If the client has a problem answering any of your questions, then that should be a red flag that maybe the job isn't for you since they're withholding info.

Back to New Orleans!

New Orleans ended up being a blast and the other models were really cool. We went to all of the hottest parties, which included numerous celebrities, several popular magazine events, and we were even go-go dancers in an Alice In Wonderland themed costumes & more themed events. It was sort of like what I would imagine Mardi

Gras to be! We even went to the opening of a very famous bar, which also had the same name as the movie! It was a blast watching the bartenders dance on the bar, the crowd went really wild. That was a great experience for my first time in New Orleans & traveling by limo wasn't too bad either. They sure know how to party in New Orleans, what a happening town! Plus, I have kept in touch with several of the Models & we have sent each other castings! What a way to network in style!

Questions I Ask Before Considering A Modeling job:

- First and last name/Name of the Company? Location of the Event or Shoot?
- Ask or a link of their work or website of their company? Ask for references, people they have worked with?
- The rate of the Assignment?
- Will here be a makeup artist/stylist/hair person provided?
- When & how you will be paid?
- Will travel, room and board be included? Will meals be included?
- How long will the assignment be? Will transportation be provided? Will you have a roommate?
- Can I see the contract ahead of time so there won't be any surprises upon arrival?

**It's always great for me to get all of this info from the client in writing, on PAPER, or in an email, just in case I have to refer back to the list later! ☺

Feel free to ask any questions, which you feel, are appropriate to feel secure about accepting the assignment! In my personal experience, I have found that an agency or two disliked that I wanted so many details of a casting, etc. Why shouldn't they be able to answer the questions I ask? Why would I want to even think about going on a casting if I don't really know what it's all about? I don't want to be surprised! I think it's important for me to know what I'm getting myself into!

X-treme Visions!

GLAMOUR GIRL CASE & POINT #4

ESPN/EXPN Summer X-Games Event
in San Francisco, CA

I received an email about the Summer X-Games Event! One of the online agencies I was with had already screened the extreme sports event client to make sure they were legit and left the rest up to me! I communicated with the client online asking questions about the assignment! Finally, he scheduled an over the phone interview and in no time, I was booked on a flight to San Francisco for a week as a spokesmodel for the extreme sports event! He forwarded me all of the details of the assignment, the name of the hotel I would be staying at, rate of the assignment, important contact information and my flight information. I was like "Oh My Goodness!" The client has never seen me in person, how crazy! This was my first online booking with traveling included, over the Internet. How exciting. It was a direct booking solely based on my most current photos and a phone interview. This is an example how the Internet can save time on castings & get you legit modeling jobs!

I had a blast in San Francisco, met a bunch of great models and we bonded easily. A few of the models, I'm still friends with today! As models, we were instructed to direct all of our charges to our rooms. Now why would they give a girl an option to charge to the room? What a bill that would be! Me, room service, and on their tab, oh my! I won't go into the details of my room bill. I'll just say that I enjoyed room service immensely & they say models don't eat! HA! I bet they were surprised! No worries, I didn't go overboard, but let's just say, the food charges were not of just salad.

Now, back to the room situation. To my surprise, my roommate ended up missing her flight and did not show up. Although I'm sure it would have been cool to meet her; my room was upgraded to a one bedroom, which was almost the top floor of the building, with one of the most amazing parnoramic views I have ever seen! There were huge floor to the ceiling windows that looked out into the city showcasing beautiful San Francisco. I felt like a Princess! The extreme sports event was amazing to watch as well. Each morning a car service took us to the location, score! It's wild when you get paid just for having fun! I loved every minute of it. Thank goodness for the World Wide Web, there are so many opportunities online!

Here is a photo of another model & I on our way to the after party for the extreme sports event! As you can see, we're all smiles and definitely having a great time.

Photo by Francois

4

Beware Of Suspicious Email Inquiries & Scams

Speaking from my personal experience, if you receive an email that has too many grammatical errors and spelling mistakes, then proceed with caution; red flag! Or maybe I'm just really picky, which is not a bad thing. Why should you proceed with caution? A girl has to have standards, right? Although I know that everyone is not the best speller in the world, a professional should make themselves look at least presentable, right? Spell-check before you send an email, its just common sense to me.

My second red flag goes up when I receive an email without the person's contact info. How am I supposed to know if you are legit if a website, location, references and further contact info is not included?

Also, it is "ALWAYS " okay to ask questions. How can you learn if you don't ask? I have learned to ask a million questions before accepting a booking, because then it makes me feel comfortable going into the photo shoot. I am a very detail oriented person, so I want all of my questions answered. If someone has a problem with this, it's a possibility that they're hiding something. Ask as many questions as you can, so there won't be any surprises.

Jamaican Me Crazy!

SCAM CASE & POINT #1

I entered a bikini contest I had heard about at an online posting. Although the contest was an hour away, the prize was an ALL-INCLUSIVE, weeklong, calendar photo shoot in Jamaica! Now that would be exciting, because I have never been to Jamaica and I've always wanted to go. Imagine: shooting with an amazing photographer for a swimsuit calendar, on an exotic island, in constant sunshine, while wearing a cute and colorful bikini…sounds perfect! The best part is that I was a winner in the contest and I was so excited!

Well, I was excited UNTIL I got the paperwork, which mentioned that I would have to pay for my own flight to & from Jamaica, which was a crazy amount at the time. What? I had WON and the prize was "ALL-INCLUSIVE! "I guess all-inclusive suddenly had a different meaning. When I called the company, they mentioned that the price was not a lot to pay for Jamaica. They went there all the time and they were giving me a great deal. I thought to myself, this was a contest, not a meeting with a travel agency. If I had wanted to pay for a trip to Jamaica for a week, I would plan to go with my friends & family. The nerve of them!

**What made me smile is that one of the photographers at the bikini contest sent me this email:

" Ivan's Comment !"

"If it means anything to ya, I was still proud of ya that you won that contest. U were the one that had all the skills anyway! A lot of those girls I thought just put on some skimpy clothes and showed as much skin as they could. Seriously a lot of those gals go there almost scared and nervous, yet you seemed like u just

walked in and you knew what had to be done. That's confidence, that's what won."

And I might add, this made things look even brighter and put a big smile on my face!

What a boost of confidence! I guess the bikini alone didn't win the contest after all!;) Hmmm...now that I think of it, I still have to plan a trip to Jamaica someday soon! I dream of that amazing island. I know I'll make it happen one day.

Dallas Gone Wild!

SCAM CASE & POINT #2

I was scheduled to do a photo shoot with a photographer in Dallas, TX. I was flown into Dallas, did the shoot, and had a great time. However, when it came time to get paid, the photographer gave me a personal check.   WRONG! NEVER take a personal check from someone. Unfortunately, the check bounced for $500. I was in shock, called the photographer and he claimed he didn't know what had happened. As if he didn't know! Needless to say, I didn't get paid for a job well done. He even had the nerve to send me the photos in the mail.   The photography was horrible. Lesson learned.

**I should have asked the photographer for a down payment before I left to Texas or a cashier's check or possibly a money order. Although I tried to pursue the matter of getting paid, taking someone to court for an out of state bounced check can be a big old' mess!

However, I was sure to warn other models on an online model message board. Little did I know, they had already badmouthed the shady photographer on this message board for taking advantage of other models. I should have done a more extensive reference check on the photographer. However, nobody is perfect! In all of my years as a model online, I have only encountered 1 bad check and 1 violation of a model release. Not bad for over 3 years online, eh?

About To Walk A Halloween Red Carpet Event!

Sin City!

SCAM CASE & POINT #3

A very popular lingerie company in town offers models a FREE trip to Las Vegas by bus for the weekend, FREE Room & Board, and a chance to be arm candy or what they call lucky charms to Casino Players!

Hmm...? There were many negatives to this situation for ME:

1. The Models would be traveling 4-5 hours on a Bus. YUCK!

2. The models would be walking around a casino in lingerie & garter belts. I don't think so!

3. The Models would be arm candy to the high rollers. As if!

4. The Models were not being paid, but had an opportunity to get paid, What?

5. The Models would be traveling back by Bus for 4-5 more hours? NO WAY!

This job was definitely not for me, so I immediately deleted it. The job seemed a little trashy to me!

However, I do know of models that attended the event and ended up making lots of money, which is totally cool for them. I'm not placing judgment on anyone, to each it's own. I just didn't feel that this job was at all appropriate for ME.

GLAMOUR GIRL TIP

Don't ever be afraid to say NO! While the Las Vegas job may be great for someone else, it wasn't for me and I felt great saying NO!

I've learned not to take every job that comes my way. It's great to BE SELECTIVE and choose jobs which best represent YOU & feels comfortable to "YOU!" YOU make the choice!

Photo by Bruce T.

5

Picture Perfect!

Only Shoot With The BEST Photographers!!

I have learned from experience to only work with the best photographers, because they know how to make me look great. I want to look my best, considering that a HUGE part of modeling that attracts clients is having a great portfolio. When I'm looking for a photographer to work with, I look at the images they have already taken of other people to see if this is the style or look I'm going after. Many photographers have their specialty that they are really good at. There are numerous types of photographers: Glamour, Swimsuit, Lingerie, Commercial, Fashion and more! Sometimes you get lucky and find a photographer that is multi-talented, because he excels in every area. After all, everyone has their specialty, which makes them shine!

GLAMOUR GIRL TIP

Believe it or not, my entire portfolio was done for FREE! I didn't pay a single cent. It is what's called a TFP, which means Time for Print. This is when a model and photographer work together and instead of payment, both receive prints to use for their books. Pretty cool, huh?

Online sites, which you can find photographers & models that may be willing to do a TFP, are:

www.modelmayhem.com

www.onemodelplace.com

Behind the Glamour!

Photoshop/Editing 101

Thank goodness for digital photography & Photoshop! Every image is now almost a perfect image, because of Photoshop and you are able to easily manipulate and create the perfect photo. You didn't really think that all of the images in magazines are exactly what the model looks like, right? "Photoshop is a Miracle Worker!"

Photoshop ERASES fine lines on the face that gives the appearance of a flawless complexion. Trust me, the models do not all look exactly like their photos. In fact some models hardly look anything like their photos if too much Photoshop & airbrushing is done. "Modeling is an illusion of perfection!" Nobody in real life is perfect, especially with no makeup on. Don't be fooled!;)

**Photoshop SMOOTHES out the skin tone. Let's face it; EVERYONE gets pimples at some point. No one is FLAWLESS! Not even a Glamour Girl like me, haha! Even if you drink gallons of water each day. Notice, in the majority of the modeling photos you see in magazines, models ALL have perfect skin. This is so not the case. Have you ever been in a live fashion show or attended one and looked at the models skin up close? Some of the models have bad skin, because they are constantly spending time in front of severe lighting conditions or they are constantly in makeup all day long, or they eat poorly or maybe they just have bad skin, perhaps all of the above! Don't be fooled.

**Added Boobies & More Body Parts courtesy of Photoshop!

Yes, I said it! A model's boobs can appear larger in photos, because boobs are added in or plumped up in Photoshop!

Or maybe the model is wearing a push up bra, miracle bra, or stuffed her bra. Believe it, it's true.

Example: I once did a shoot with a fabulous photographer. I absolutely ADORED his photos, because of the great lighting and the way the models all looked so mannequin-like They ALL looked like Barbie Dolls! Little did I know, I was his next project. When I got the photos back, I stared at them, because I did not even recognize myself! I sat at the computer screen reviewing the images wondering, "Who is this Girl?" Although it was me, I didn't recognize myself, because suddenly my B boobs had gone to a D, my nose was suddenly thinner, there was extra hair added onto my own hair, and my cheekbones had disappeared, because they had been airbrushed away! Who was I? LOL! ☺ I even called my friends over and asked them if the photos looked like me. It was such a drastic change in appearance that even I was clueless! I know this sounds funny, but it's true. Sometimes, Photoshop can be overdone taken a bit far. Don't you think? Personally, I find an image more appealing when the person looks at least a bit realistic, not like a videogame character. Although videogame characters are great. LOL! ☺ In fact, my body was scanned for a videogame once, it was a neat experience!

I have also found that a photographer who has mastered the art of lighting is one that I want to work with. He or She is a TRUE CHAMPION! Photography is all about the right lighting. After all, a clear, sharp image, with great lighting is what I want since I am the subject and want to look my best.

Also, it is great to present excellent photos of yourself, because many times clients may not have time to see you in person and they book you strictly off of what your photos, headshot or model comp card images.

Be sure to include on your model card:

- A smiling photo!
- A 3/4-length image!
- A full-length image showcasing your body from head to toe!
- A headshot!

Most importantly, put your realistic stats! With all of this in hand, you're prepared and armed for success in the modeling world!

And speaking of REALISTIC STATS! I have heard so many horror stories of models giving photographers fake measurements. Why lie when they are going to have to see you in person at some point and see that you're not at all what you say? It will only make you look silly when you show up and possibly waste the photographers time, because he/she just may send you home for being dishonest. Okay, so I know models may fib about their height at times, but that can sometimes be easily fixed with a great pair of high heels! Ha-ha!

Speaking of weight issues. I get plenty of emails asking me about my workout plan & if I diet? NO way do I workout or diet. However, I do stay active. I must thank my parents for giving me excellent genes. I also have NEVER dieted! I eat whatever I want and in moderation. I basically eat 5 small meals a day or more, instead of huge meals 3 times a day like most people. Huge meals just make me feel gross & sleepy. So eating throughout the day keeps me happy & full! ☺

GLAMOUR GIRL SECRET

However, one photographer told me that a model showed up at the shoot 20 pounds heavier than she had mentioned in their conversation & stated on her model card. He was completely shocked, because it was such a big difference that he didn't even bother to do the photo shoot with her. Feel good about yourself, be proud of your weight, and tell the TRUTH about your weight if you're going to be a Model! "The truth shall set you free!"

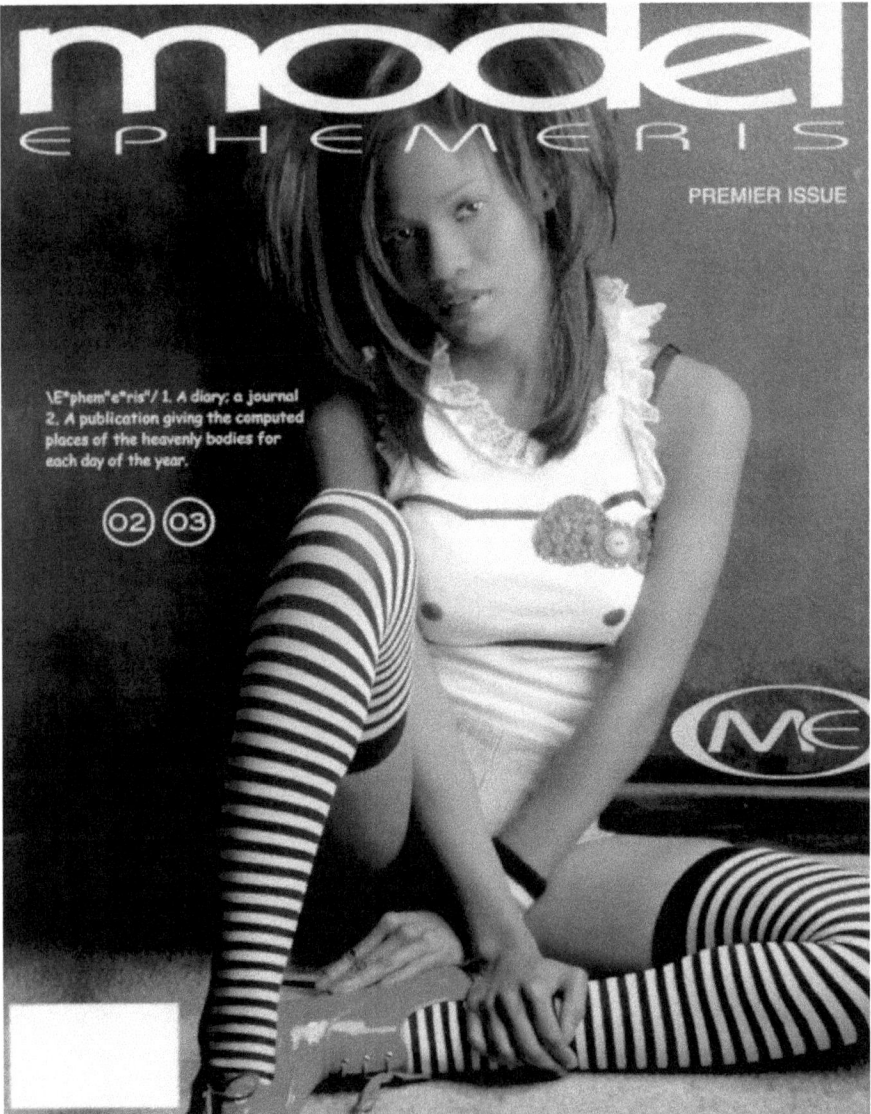

Woo-hoo, I'm a Cover Model for the Premiere Issue of
Model Ephemeris Magazine!!

Photo by Rondell S.

6

Follow the Leader!

Follow Directions

I received an email from a popular video game company! They were looking for models to scan for a new game they were creating. Wow, the possibility of being a videogame character seemed really cool. The submission process consisted of me sending a full-length digital photo, standing, facing the camera, arms out a bit, and legs apart a bit via email. Then a side-view photo showing my profile. Simple directions, right? WRONG! Well, after booking the job, I found out not only did I have the right body dimensions they were looking for, but also I seemed to be the only one who had followed directions. They received submissions of models that were not full-length. People sent in photos with their heads cut off. What? I thought. Those were simple directions. They were simple directions that others did not follow and this is also one of the reasons I booked the job. The company even started to send other models examples of my photos, so they knew what to send in. I was a perfect example of what they had asked for. The shoot ended up being so much fun.

Barker's Beauty!

GLAMOUR GIRL CASE & POINT #5

Okay, so of course I'm not perfect. In fact, NOBODY is Perfect! Don't let anyone tell you differently. One of my online agencies sent me on an audition for a huge television show that's been on for years & I was so excited. I was told to wear a bathing suit, walk down to the end of the hallway, and shake the persons hand at the end. Simple, right? So what did I do? Even though I've seen the popular TV show a million times & knew what to do, guess what happened? I wore my bathing suit proudly, while bouncing happily down the hallway, and on the way I said "HERE I COME" shook the guys hand and returned back down the hallway!

You're wondering, "What was my mistake?" Well, if you watch the popular TV show, the girls DO NOT SPEAK AT ALL. They just walk around smiling and making hand gestures. Silly me, I just had to talk, which actually meant that maybe that wasn't the perfect job for me anyway, because I love to talk! HA-HA! This could have been the reason I didn't book the job. I'm not sure if this really was the reason or maybe I was just clearly not what they were looking for. I guess maybe I would have booked the job if the "Price Is Right?"

"Laugh & Get Rich!!"
A book by Rick Segel & Darren La Croix

42

Cover Model for the *Blend of Beauty Calendar*
Photo by Tony S.

Photo by Stars for *FHM* Magazine

7

Have Fun.

They'll Remember You & Book You For More Work

GLAMOUR GIRL CASE & POINT #6

People work with people they like and have fun with! How do I know this? It's been proven over and over again. Let's take for example the video game booking I was telling you about earlier. Everyone was pretty quiet during the shoot. Silence filled the room. I'm thinking, this is a video game company; it should be a fun & upbeat atmosphere, right? Plus it was just too silent in the room for me. Being quite the comedian that I am, I started to say in a silent voice "It's so quiet in here," which immediately broke the ice and everyone burst out laughing. The shoot was only a couple of hours, but the time flew by, because I used a little humor to shake things up a bit, while still getting the job done.

How do I know that my natural technique of humor worked? When the next model arrived, one of the producers whispered to me, "He looks a little bit shy, I bet it won't be as much fun as working with you!" Hearing this totally brought a smile to my face, because I had made a memorable stay, because I had fun with the job. I had made a great impression. Now that I think back, the day was even better, because the shoot ended up going overtime for many reasons and I was paid more, EXCELLENT! A job well done. Plus the video game company booked me again, but this time they scanned my face for the videogame. How cool! This time the shoot was for less time & more money. SCORE!

Bench Warmer Trading Card Model!
Photo by Dan Peterson!

Personality Plus!

GLAMOUR GIRL CASE & POINT #7

On my website, I added a diary section to showcase my personality a little bit more and well to be perfectly honest, it's because I love writing. Could this be the reason I'm writing this book? Hmmm?? Okay back to the reason I added the diary to my website. Sometimes I think I may come off looking a bit serious in my photos or unapproachable, but this is so not true about me. I'm outgoing, love to go out, spontaneous and enjoy making people smile. My journal included event photos, photo shoot outtakes, smiling photos, party pictures, personal photos, and even photos taken by myself with my digital camera. Maybe it's a blessing that I don't know how to use Photoshop, because my snapshot photos are the REAL ME, untouched, just the raw image. What you see is what you get.

That lovable diary of mine ends up booking me more work than I had imagined. Why? I constantly have updated snapshots of my current look. In real life, outside of modeling photos, I hardly wear makeup, so they can get a better idea of what I look like without so much makeup on from modeling. I constantly receive emails saying how much personality comes through in my diary entries, how friendly I appear, and therefore more visitors to my site, which is fantastic, because people want to read what I'm up to next. COOL! Did you notice how the word FUN came up? Remember: people work with people who are fun, nice, and easy to work with! Cha-Ching!;)

"Everyone you encounter is either helping you get where you want to go or preventing you from getting there. There are no neutral people in your life."

Rick Butts from the book "The Big Butts of Life!"

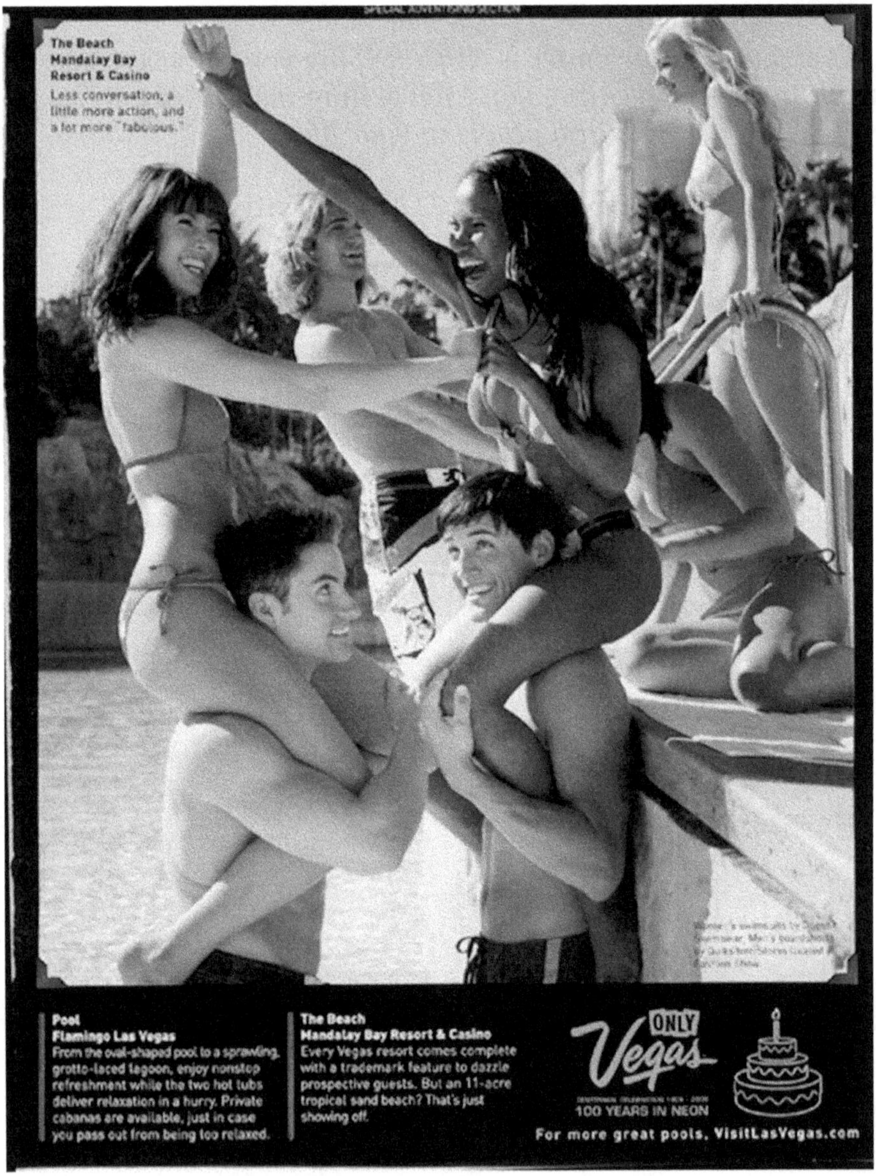

Las Vegas Anniversary Ad for *Maxim* Magazine

8

Surround Yourself With People...
Who Believe In You & Support Your Career!!

I cannot begin to tell you how important it is to surround yourself with POSITIVITY! I am lucky enough to have friends and family that show me so much support and rewards for my accomplishments with modeling as well as everything else I do.

Okay, so maybe it didn't start out this way. Especially since I moved from Washington, after graduating college, with a Degree in Political Science to Los Angeles, CA to become a model. I think my family went into shock when I told them my plans. They kept trying to tempt me and tell me how they would pay for my law school, buy me a car, and other fine materialistic items, which seem great in order for me to continue my education instead of moving to L.A. to become a model. Of course, I followed my heart & moved to L.A.!

"If you follow your own plans & dreams and don't let anyone talk you out of them, then you'll start to get the hang of being an heiress!"

Paris Hilton / Confessions of an Heiress

Stay Goal Oriented!

However, I had a GOAL & a PLAN, I knew that I wanted to be a model or at least try. I even created a diary of several positive and negative experiences along my path to becoming a successful model, which was my motivation whenever I needed a pick me upper.

When I started to send home magazines, calendars, and books I had been published in, my family and friends were so excited and proud of me. YAY! My mother had finally seen that I was doing what I truly loved as well as enjoyed. I was actually living my dream! I made it happen! To this day, it makes me so happy whenever my Mom reminds me that she has folders where she keeps all of my modeling accomplishments in, so cool. The other day she called me in the middle of the day, because she was at the newsstand looking to buy the magazine I was currently in. Imagine that! How cool, that makes me so happy! It honestly brought a huge smile to my face.

"The journey to finding your true self
takes a commitment to keep going no matter what.
Keep going despite your feelings.
Keep taking action despite your fears.
Keep focusing on your journey, the process. If you do, the
results will take care of themselves."

Rhonda Britten/Life Coach
from the TV series "Starting Over"

It's a GREAT IDEA to Stay Motivated about what your goals are in life! The people surrounding you should totally be 100% supportive and helping you reach your goals, dreams, and aspirations. Let's be honest, not everyone is happy and upbeat all the time and self-motivated and they may need a pep talk every now and then to get them back on track. This is when the people surrounding you, should come in handy even more to guide you along the way.

"The number 1 reason people fail to achieve their potential is the people they choose to hang around with!"

Rick Butts / The Big Butts of Life book!

Bikini Contest Winner!
I'm posing with a lifeguard on the beach
of an all expense paid trip to Cancun, Mexico!!

Fun In The Sun!!

GLAMOUR GIRL CASE & POINT #8

A friend of mine emailed me a flyer he had seen online for a bikini contest & suggested that I enter. I remember that I didn't want to enter the bikini contest, at a nearby venue, because you now how they usually select girls with big boobs, more curvaceous figures, blonde, blah, blah, blah. I had decided that I wasn't going to enter and my friend practically carried me there. He picked me up and dropped me off, so there was no way for me to run back home. Well I guess I could have taken a cab! LOL!☺ I stayed, smiled, did my walk down the runway twice and what do you now, I placed in the contest and WON an all expenses paid trip to Cancun, Mexico for a week and I had an blast! I could have missed out on a great opportunity if my friend didn't cheer me on & convince me to go. Your TRUE FRIENDS should have your BEST interest in mind at ALL TIMES!!

"My best friend is the one who
brings out the best in me!"
Henry Ford

JET Beauty 2004 1ˢᵗ Ever Swimsuit Calendar!!

Copyright of Johnson Publishing Company
Photo by James Mitchell

Beauty of the Week!!

GLAMOUR GIRL CASE & POINT #9

Ever since I was a little girl, I had seen JET Magazine and I always thought how cool it would be to be JET Beauty of the Week. After getting an email from my friend about submissions for being a JET Beauty of the Week, I went to the website and sent in my photos to the appropriate email. Well, what do you know, my dream came true and I became that Jet Beauty of the Week. Thanks to my friend who was looking out for me. Have you ever noticed that some people procrastinate and make excuses for themselves, but they never APPLY themselves? Hmmm?? My friend sent me info on how to be in JET Magazine's first ever calendar "JET BEAUTY!" I read the email and saved it. (Procrastination) Then one day, as I was clearing out my email, I noticed that the day I was reading the email was the deadline date. Oh NO! I quickly put together my submission and headed off to the post office to mail in my entry. What the heck, right? Why not try? Well, what do you know, I ended up being selected for the calendar, flown to Chicago and did a photo shoot for the first ever JET Beauty Calendar! I was so excited! By my girlfriend sending me the submission info, I was able to further my JET Magazine dream as a child as well as appear in the calendar. Yay!☺ Another dream accomplished! See what happens when you surround yourself with positive people, YOU APPLY yourself & take ACTION? Great things are bound to happen!

Political Science & Criminal Justice Degree ... Law School Bound!

GLAMOUR GIRL CASE & POINT #10

I've realized a lot of my examples throughout the book have been titled Case & Point! Is this because I could have gone to law school and my pre-law courses are kicking in? LOL ☺ One of my fans of my website sent me a box full of motivational books for my birthday, I was so excited! Because of these books, I became even more inspired to write my own motivational books for others to read and hopefully become inspired!

"Your companions are like the buttons on an elevator. They will either take you up, or they will take you down!"
Unknown

Super Crew = Super Model!

GLAMOUR GIRL CASE & POINT #11

It is really phenomenal to have a website, because with my experience, I receive so many positive and motivational emails that are awesome every single day. I could be having a bad day or maybe feeling a bit unmotivated and a simple email can totally get me back on track and bring a huge smile to my face. My fan support is phenomenal!

FANS & Mentors ROCK!!!!

One of my Mentors "JIM, who is a Teacher from South Carolina sends me motivational emails each week as well as really cool positive quotes! We've become GREAT friends. Jim's like a COACH, constantly cheering me on! He rewards me every time I advance in my modeling career! During my modeling career, fans have sent me gifts including a digital camera, which I use to capture behind the scenes photos from my modeling photo shoots & fun party photos as well as to record behind the scene clips from my modeling shoots, a ton of wardrobe, which I have used to wear in my photo shoots & most recently items to assist & prepare me for my travels! As to my mentor, Jim, what a great guy & such a positive person, his students are so lucky! ☺ THANKS, JIM! ☺

Another Fan sends me tons of motivational books from the printing company he works at, because he knows that I love to write. I absolutely love books and it reminded me of my love of reading and writing. The books have been a huge inspiration in helping me to complete this book! ☺

Another Fan: JOHN sends me postcards from all of the places he travels to, because he knows of my dreams of traveling the world. When I see the postcards and he describes his experiences, it's as if I were traveling right along with him. Thanks John!;)

I am very lucky to have such supportive fans that believe in me and inspire me to be the best I can be! ☺ To all of my FANS, I salute You!

> *"A genuine friend encourages & challenges*
> *us to live out our best thoughts, honor our*
> *purest motives, & achieve our*
> *most significant dreams!"*
> Dan Reiland

Beyond Your Wildest Dreams!

GLAMOUR GIRL CASE & POINT #12

I have a friend, who also happens to be a photographer, who always talks to me as if I can honestly accomplish "Absolutely" anything my heart desires. His dreams for me are often times beyond what I personally have in mind, which helps me to strive for even more. He makes me laugh every time he says "Just wave at me from the limo!" He's so funny! Once we were about to go out for coffee, tea for me. I didn't have on any makeup and looked super casual, totally not a picture perfect moment. As I walked out of the door, he snapped a candid photo of me. I was like "No He Didn't!" When he moved out of the country, he later sent that photo to me and written on the back, it said, "Shantelle, caught by paparazzi!" He's so funny! He also gave me all of his cool photography and model books before he moved. I was in heaven, some of my favorite books that I've always wanted. Thanks for the inspiration Francois, you rock! ☺ I miss you!

My Friends ROCK...
they always bring out the best in me!

Front row!

GLAMOUR GIRL CASE & POINT #13

I have a cute, super colorful, little flowery yellow bag that I got from L.A. Fashion Week. I was representing a website as a Reporter to do behind the scenes interviews with designers, celebrities, & models! I even got the chance to interview one of my favorite designers, Daniella Clarke of Frankie B.! I love Frankie B. Jeans! Low-waist jeans are my favorite. I was given a VIP pass to sit in the front row at numerous fashion shows during the entire Fashion Week, what a blast! The gift bags were amazing, plenty of girl stuff: hair products, makeup, magazines, clothes, purses, gift certificates, and more! In this cute little flowery bag, I keep my motivational articles which include: Magazine Cutouts, Positive Articles, Inspirational Quotes, Photos, and more which motivates me to follow my dreams. I love reading about how people became successful and how they accomplished their life long goals.

Book Smart!

I also keep a Personal Journal that uses language that speaks my dreams. I use certain words that drive my dreams home. I think it's very important to PLAN ON PAPER, because it's concrete evidence as a reminder of your goals. It's also important to make small and big goals, and be sure to reward yourself for goals accomplished. It feels great when you check them off or cross them out for a job well done.

I keep a collection of positive quotes that I receive in my email from friends, family, & fans to look at when I need a bit of encouragement or a confidence booster.

I also subscribe to "Chicken Soup For The Soul" emails! They are free inspirational stories, which always bring a smile to my face and leaves me full with positivity!

www.dailyinbox.com

I also made a list of long and short-term goals on a piece of bright yellow paper as a constant reminder of my personal goals. Since I love COLOR, the pretty color paper makes me want to keep looking at the list over & over.

I love reading this really cool book by Essence Magazine called "Making it Happen! Creating Success and Abundance!" The book is edited by Patricia M. Hinds. What a great book with tons of inspirational stories and how each person became successful, including well-known celebrities.

I cut out articles in magazines by celebrities or people that I'm inspired by. I love knowing how people became successful. I love studying their backgrounds and hearing their personal stories, which in turn inspires me. If they can do it, so can I!

** I can't tell you how many times I've read this article I found in Cosmo Magazine from June 1999 *Visualize It! The Little Trick That Lets You Land Your Dream Life!"* by Rosie Amodio, (pages 177-179).

It totally helps, I swear! That article has helped me make several changes in my life over and over again!

I'm also signed up to get Oprah's Mission Calendar by email, it's a newsletter, which has daily positive, inspirational, quotes that really can make a difference and get you motivated! www.oprah.com

I'm also signed up to get one positive quote a day at www.positivepress.com & www.goal-setting-guide.com

It's so cool to know that each day that I sign in to check my email, a positive quote will be there to make me smile! ☺

I enjoy watching what I call "SMART GIRL MOVIES!" These are movies such as "Legally Blonde 1 & 2!" I love both movies, because the character is a very SMART GIRL who gets an education, graduates from law school, and has fun along the way. Everyone things she's a ditz, because she's completely into her wardrobe, always wants to make things pretty, and wants to make the world a better place, but she always finishes first at the top of her class proving them all wrong! Plus at the end, it has a really cute music video & song by LeAnn Rimes titled "You Can Do The Impossible!" I love it! You do know that you can be a total GLAMOUR GIRL as well as a SMART GIRL at the same time, just multi-task & smile big! They'll never even see you coming!

It's also very important to study your craft, whatever it is that you want to do! I study model poses from magazines, read as many as books as possible as a reminder of what my goals are and how to be an expert in my field of modeling as well as writing. It's important to continue educating yourself! There is always time to learn something new as well as keep your mind active.

9

My Best Accessories!

Have A Backup Plan/Get An Education

Yes, it is true that after graduating college, instead of going to law school, I decided to move to L.A. and become a Model. Yes, I know it sounds crazy & my parents were like, what? Keep in mind, I'm a true believer in following your heart and making your "OWN" dreams come true. You NEVER have to prove anything in life to anyone, that's just too exhausting & takes up too much time for the things you TRULY want to do. Just do what makes YOU happy, whatever is fulfilling & rewarding to you. Life is what YOU make it! If you desire to do something, get out there and make it happen. What are you waiting for? Life gives us a blank piece of paper each day, get out there & write your OWN story. Come on, I know you can do it, if you just give it a try!

I know you're like "Where did all of this positive, shiny, energy come from?" I guess it's from my days as a cheerleader while in college. You have to be your own cheerleader in life and go after whatever you want in life. I will always have my University degree in Political Science to fall back on! I know that I won't be a model forever. Looks can fade but intelligence is FOREVER!! Wait a minute, what am I saying? I live in L.A., the capital of the world for plastic surgery; maybe looks can be forever for the right price, haha! I'm all for "Whatever Makes You Happy!" Do whatever makes you feel good inside! YOU be the judge! And by the way, plastic surgery is so not for me, it's a personal choice to be natural!;)

BE REALISTIC!!

While modeling can bring in a lot of dough, it doesn't always. Have other goals in life. Don't quit your day job in hopes that modeling will pay the bills, because 9 times out of 10 that doesn't happen. Well, unless you're on the same level as Cindy Crawford, Iman, or Naomi Campbell. Follow your dreams, but be realistic about your goals. Dream BIG but live in the real world as well and have a PLAN. I haven't always been a model forever. Trust me, I have had plenty of jobs before becoming a model: Retail, a Restaurant, Movie Theater, TV Station, Radio Station, Music Video Company as a casting director, and I could go on and on. Hmm…have you noticed that most of the jobs, with the exception of the restaurant have been in the field of Entertainment? Maybe I knew what I truly wanted to do from the start.

Always on the go & on a mission to travel the world!

10

"Coast to Coast....From 1 Girl 2 Another!"
Network, Network, Network!!

A great way to drive in more traffic to your website is to link up to other like-minded websites & people. Since fashion is my passion, I linked up with other model sites, modeling sites, magazine sites, makeup sites, photography sites, sites which feature you on their sites, submit to search engines, and more online destinations. There are so many ways to promote your modeling career and be seen on the web.

Three Great Sites To Check Out:

1. www.onemodelplace.com

*This site gets over 2 million hits a day, lets you create a free page with your 5 photos, your stats, modeling/acting interests, resume, and a link to your personal site. They also offer PAID Membership, which includes further exposure to job castings, message boards, and a higher search engine ranking.

Several of the modeling websites have great articles that taught me the rules of gaining great exposure on the web and allow for maximum exposure.

2. www.models.com

*This is a great site to be seen by today's top modeling agencies! Why you ask? The agencies have interviews on this website, look for talent on this site, and there are many helpful modeling hints on how to become a model, along with success stories!

Keep a Mailing List:

**This will inform your fans of any new additions to your website, brand new photos, if you're added a new item to your store, or any news at all you would like to share with them to keep them coming back to your site!

3. www.mailchimp.com

Mail Chimp is a free website offering free mailing list scripts as well as many other fun additions to any website!

I could list a million and one online websites, but that would take forever, just get online and explore! In fact, once you're already on a few modeling websites and appear in search engines, you will start to get email from numerous websites wanting to feature you or put you on their site for free. ALL exposure is GREAT exposure! Right? This just drives more traffic to your site, a chance to be seen, and possibly paid modeling work for you. ☺

Cyber Connections

GLAMOUR GIRL CASE & POINT #14

A book publisher from my hometown in Washington contacted me online to be one of the cover model and featured model inside of his cookbook. At the photo shoot I met the makeup artist who later showed my photos to Lowrider. I ended up booking a photo shoot for Lowrider Magazine and was in a feature for their tribute to 9/11. One of the models from the cookbook I shot the cover with invited me to be on her bikini team and booked me to be in a major runway show, which included wearing diamonds. This same model told me about an audition for four spokesmodels for an upcoming tour, which would travel throughout the United States, including making TV and radio appearances. Well, what do you know! I ended up booking the tour as a spokesmodel and traveled all over the US, imagine that! All of this happened through one single online contact. Each experience was amazing as well as financially rewarding, I might add.

Tearsheets from *Nokia* ad and
Lowrider Magazine 9/11 Tribute

11

Make Your Dreams Come 2 Life!

Have fun on the World Wide Web.
There are plenty of opportunities.

My friend reminds me every single time that I get an online booking of me saying "That's not going to work!" Why did I ever say that about the Internet? But thank goodness, I took a CHANCE and went online! You never know unless you try, right? Without the Internet, I may have never had the many traveling, modeling, and networking opportunities. I have been able to find online & offline agencies to represent me as well as book me. I secured a booking with a particular video game client online, because I had a digital camera and was able to take snapshots of myself to send immediately. The Internet has also proved to be a major time saver for both myself and the client booking models online. I didn't have to spend time and gas money driving to a casting and they didn't have to wait for me to get there, PERFECT! I do know that TIME is money and no one has time for you to waste their money. I have also enjoyed traveling the USA and several times out of the country to Mexico for modeling at a charity event. Luckily, my experiences online have been awesome and taken me all over the place. I have been able to travel to several exotic places and attend cool events, because a company looking for models saw my work online at www.Shantelle.net

I believe that the Internet is a great place for models that are not the traditional industry standard 5′9 to gain exposure to make their modeling dreams come true! My body just happens to be very proportionate, don't let the long legs fool ya'! LOL! ☺ I am nowhere near 5′9 or even 5′8. There are many avenues for models at all different heights, shapes, and sizes! So, get out there & turn your dream into a reality, Start "TODAY" and make it happen! Don't wait another moment! Like the VERIZON Wireless slogan says "Make Progress Everyday!"

That's a WRAP… Until next time! Follow your dreams. If I can, so can you! Start TODAY!

A Few of My Model Resume Favorites:

- MAXIM Magazine
- Miller Lite (print ad)
- FHM Magazine
- Nokia (print ad)
- Las Vegas Anniversary (print ad)
- JET Magazine (Beauty of the Week)
- JET Beauty Swimsuit Calendar (1ˢᵗ ever)
- Blockbuster Video Box (Cover Model)
- Sophisticate's Black Hair Magazine
- Lowrider Magazine (Centerfold Model/9/11 Tribute)
- Lowrider Magazine (Featured Model & Confessions book interview)
- Rangefinder Magazine
- The Beauty of Fetish: Volume II (book)
- Bench Warmer Trading Cards (Featured Model)
- Columbia Caller I.D. Box (Cover Model)
- Blend of Beauty Calendar (Cover Model)
- L.A. Fashion Week (Reporter)
- The Lingerie Bowl (Cheerleader & Spokesmodel on Tour throughout the USA)
- The Player's Run (Spokesmodel on Tour)
- Black Men's Magazine (Feature Model)
- G4 Video Game TV Attack of the Show (Model)
- World Poker Classic Tournament (Spokesmodel)
- Numerous tradeshows, books, calendars, charity events & more!

**The Resume listed was made possible by having my photos online at www.SHANTELLE.NET !!

Shantelle

ABOUT THE AUTHOR

Shantelle is a former model and university graduate; current Author, Traveler, Entrepreneur & Lover of Life!

She enjoys traveling & has traveled to 14 countries & 4 continents so far! She has a passion for travel and experiencing new cultures as well as meeting new people along the way. Her enthusiasm for travel has inspired others via her photographs as well as the stories she tells. Shantelle's books have an inspirational/motivational theme to bring out the best from the reader within.

She enjoys living by the beach in sunny Southern California, as she's a true beach lover. Shantelle believes in living life to the fullest as well as inspiring others to take action & follow their dreams!

She also loves reading, writing, roller coasters, collecting positive quotes, milk chocolate, grape leaves & going to the movies...and smiles & laughs often! Shantelle lives life with pure enthusiasm & is always in the attitude of gratitude! Visit her website at: www.Shantelle.net & follow her travels at www.JetSetDreams.com

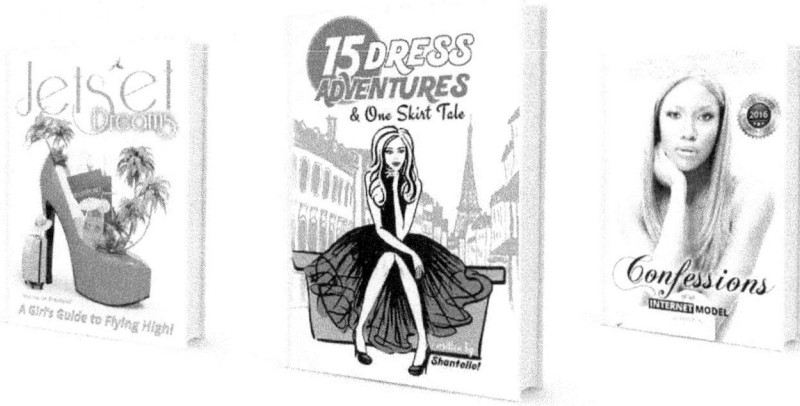

Other Books by Shantelle!

Jet Set Dreams: A Girl's Guide to Flying High

15 Dress Adventures & One Skirt Tale

Shantelle